THE WHOLE NIGHT, COMING HOME

Due

ALSO BY ROO BORSON

Landfall   1977
In the Smoky Light of the Fields   1980
Rain   1980
Night Walk   1981
A Sad Device   1981
The Transparence of November / Snow
  (with Kim Maltman)   1984

Roo Borson

THE WHOLE NIGHT, COMING HOME

McCLELLAND AND STEWART

The Canadian Publishers
McClelland and Stewart Limited
481 University Avenue
Toronto, Ontario M5G 2E9

Canadian Cataloguing in Publication Data

Borson, Roo, 1952–
    The whole night, coming home

Poems.
ISBN 0-7710-1579-8

I. Title.

PS8553. 0786W56 1984   C811'.54   C84-098771-4
PR9199.3.B67W56

The publisher makes grateful acknowledgement to the Ontario Arts Council and the Canada Council for their assistance.

Set in Sabon by The Typeworks, Vancouver
Printed and bound in Canada by Gagné Ltd.

For Mom & Dad,
Dave, Soo, Benj,
and for Kim

CONTENTS

LIGHTS FOR KIM

Here on the hill as the lights begin to come on –
that sweet dampness next to the earth
and the haunted feeling
that it's all built on nothing,
hills gouged with the light of gas stations, and streets,
those luminous grey crosses that taper into the distance.

Tonight I can't look at you
without seeing how our faces are put together
of weaknesses. And beyond that
of rock dust, finally
of extinct shapes no longer known to the earth.

A motorcycle disappearing into the hills:
the sound drifts up and up with no end.

Because of those strange depths marked by stars
the world gets stuck in the throat
and I see the look in your eyes that shows you
crossing the bright floor of your solitary house
when it is night outside, though you are in my arms.

Across the bay the downtown
is a billboard of empty buildings with their lights on,
buildings that don't know what it is we're after,
that just stand there, letting themselves be built
and then knocked down.
An airplane takes a low running start and then lifts
with the grace of a planned thing.
Sequences of lamps fluorescing into distance,
the curve of shore home for nothing but dark brilliant weeds.

Fit your heartbeat against the empty side of my chest,
close your eyes. Conversation is fuel
like I'm a kid again, scrawling a few awkward spirals
because no one has taught us to make the real words yet.

FLYING LOW

I

THE WHOLE NIGHT, COMING HOME

Low white garden fences, glossy leaves
of camellia and lemon after rain.
After dinner, walking, just for a breath
of air away from the family.
The Johnstons' yard glistens
though it's not theirs anymore.
Someone else lives there. Still
they're Nick Johnston's lemon trees.

The firs, their shaggy branches full of rain.
The big rock where all the kids used to play,
building forts around it. Now
it's haunted, more than empty.

Through the mist, the clearing rain,
the whole city blinks like a jet on a runway.
You can hear the engines rev, forever, going nowhere.

The bench that used to look out over it,
where we sat for hours, for those few years,
trying out kisses on first lovers: this time
it's gone. Four marks in the ground.
And the eucalyptus trees
still fluttering over it, with stars between the leaves.

We could own anything then,
just by being there when the owners were asleep.
We had the whole city, the whole night.
It's possible to come back
but none of it's yours anymore. It belongs
to someone else. But where are they?
Asleep like their parents? Or have they found
new places, places you don't know how to find
because you don't need them enough anymore.

It's so hot you can hear
insects dropping from the trees and the crickets
playing the cracked violins of their bodies in the long grass.
And so the moon creeps up over the hillside
in a surprise attack, running in rivulets
down the sides of buildings, smothering the shadows
in a rash of white violets.
Only the pines have the stamina
to hold their starlike needles inert
as the sparks of meteors cascade through them.
It's so hot that just to lie there
burns the soles of your feet, you walk on a desert of air
lying perfectly still. Thousands of grains of oxygen
sucked in and out of your nostrils as you breathe.
It would be better if there were someone
lying next to you, but you're not old enough for that yet.
And when moonlight soaks the fissures of grass
you imagine the grasshoppers
fucking there.
It's so hot you get up and the floor
crackles with little pockets of air under the linoleum
as you bring the cool washcloth to lay across your feet
and get back into bed. It's not a night for sleeping
but for remembering what it will be like
years from now, remembering this.
It wouldn't seem so hot with someone lying next to you.
It won't ever seem this hot again.

Stepping outside, shutting the door. The night air
full of jasmine and the sound of traffic, windy, distant,
people on their own, going places.
Under bare feet the grass is cool, almost damp.
Nothing to do. Only you can't stay inside, in the livingroom
where your family bloats in the undersea light of the TV
or the empty room upstairs which is yours.
Starting up the hill behind the house, the crickets close by
stop suddenly. So you walk in a moving spotlight
of silence.

The hills behind you are a dark wake.
Where you've stopped to sit the crickets
stay stiff, alert near the roots of grass.
On the left a fan of searchlights opens a fake aurora.
Further off the crickets rattle brightly under the straw,
their music marked with sudden breaks
and new beginnings. Maybe you came to see the deer,
the trampled ovals where they've lain – how many of them? –
     together,
but they never come, not while you're near. Tonight,
any night, you don't know why you've come, only
that there's nowhere else to be.
                      Looking down across the bay,
a long arm's reach away the city streams
like a brilliant plasma, a piece of human tissue.
What does this mean? It means
too many things, all tangled together.
The licorice of Queen Anne's lace,
the nothing smell of clean earth,
the sharp resin of raw lumber: someone you've never met
building on the hilltop. Brambles
the deer will feed on when you're finally

asleep in the house again. Raccoons
will drink from the pond in the garden, leaving
dark forked prints in the mud. Everything
will begin again once you've gone inside. Only tonight
maybe you'll stay up here on the hill.
Maybe you just won't bother going in ever again.

BLACKBERRIES

The eucalyptus shadows hang
like knives, knives that cut nothing,
shadows. A breeze starts up
like a little thrill
going through a crowd. The wet smoke smell.
A shadow shivers over the hills
and the two girls still picking blackberries
down in the bushes stop and listen.
They've been told about this wind. They've been told
it can get you pregnant, that in the dark spaces
between bushes sometimes a man crouches.
That at the sight of a girl a man
just goes crazy, he can't help himself.
They keep picking, but faster. All they want
is some blackberries. Their mothers tell them that someday
they'll get more than they bargained for
staying out this late. They know they should be going.
But the sun leaks out again, dimly,
then floods over the bushes, over their hands and faces,
a heat which turns their skin white again
and sparkles on the leaves. The blackberries
are taut and warm and sweet; the kernels shine
like the thoraxes of solitary ants making their way
across the dirt. The girls have a game
with sunlight, they pretend
it makes them invisible. But around their mouths
and on their fingers the ragged pink stains
will take a long, long time to go away.

The wind. It comes at night,
trying to claw the house apart.
It goes at all the windows.
The windows shudder in their frames.
The wind wants you to come out and be blown
forever through a world moving too fast
for you to see it. The way the wind sees it.
So what if you lie under the covers and shiver?
The same wind goes through your lungs, through and through . . .
through and through.

DIVINATION

Bright sun flashing off windshields: mirrors everywhere.
Dusty oaks
stake their shadows to the hillsides,
their dark crooked reflections.

When a child rides through a tunnel
he has to press his head against the back seat
to count the lights that flick past overhead. And he has
to be ready: he can't let that blackness
with its terrifying lights take him by surprise
but it always does. He misses the first few
and then starts counting like mad because he believes
everything he's told – he has to.
That the lights show how long his mother has to live.
That leaves it up to him,
to how fast he can count without moving his lips –
no cheating – and his mother right there in the front seat.
He always forgets how many he counted
the last time, but no matter. Things can change.
It's a huge feeling.

And the children walking to school after rain:
they have to be careful. They stretch their short legs
and practically hop from one foothold to the next,
finding the spaces to put a shoe down
between the cracks in the sidewalk and the long
pink worms that come up as if from another world
and lie like spaghetti everywhere.

But today is Saturday, and the teenagers
are riding around in their cars at dusk.
Now that they're old enough
to not know what to do with themselves
from one minute to the next

their parents start asking
what they're going to do with the rest of their lives.
The oak trees won't tell them.
The oaks are lost in their own dim world.

So the teenagers ride around in cars with friends,
sometimes going places, sometimes saying nothing,
lying back just gazing
at the rate of ten years per second
at the horizon. Amazing how it manages to tell nothing.

THE WAYS WE'RE TAUGHT

So he takes her to a place in the hills where he
thinks she'll give in to him.
That's what he's been taught:
girls can't resist pretty things.
So he shows her how the lights
shine through the trees
and then undoes his pants.
That's what they've been taught,
the girl to let herself be taken
so far and then say no, the boy
to try for anything.
The hills just lie there like rumpled velvet,
and the skull of the moon floats out of them.
This is what it is to be fifteen
and not know what to make of being alive.
The party was loud. If you drink a little
the music takes care of everything,
it lifts you off the floor, dancing forward
at unknown miles an hour until somebody
falls down and has to be dragged outside.
It's easy to drink too much,
to let it all get away with you.
There's always somebody who never learns
what a bottle and a couple of pills can do.
Still, they've always woken up, telling the story
of how beautiful the tall cool trees look
when you're falling backwards.
So nobody's too shaken up,
somebody thinks to put on another record
and keep dancing. Feelings,
they run so much smoother
when they're riding on the notes
of somebody else's song.
It's easier to feel anything

once it's been said before.
The girls, they're all looking around
for a boy who'll give them anything,
and the boys know it, they've been taught
to take what they can get.
So he offers her a ride home.
He says he'll show her something along the way.

SIXTEEN

All night she's lain listening to the rain
dropping like small change into puddles.
Trying to lie still beside the boy.

Now it's cold outside, grey and dripping from the eaves.
Each step seems to lift her
a foot off the ground from lack of sleep.
The houses – soaked through and strangely bright.
A cat prances up sideways
then scoots off through the bushes
deep in its own wildness.

The high school where they both go:
the fence pulled shut with a chain.
She can smell the hamburger places:
heat, grease, fresh donuts.
A smell vaguely like fog, vaguely like coffee.
The traffic lights go from gold to red to green
and back again.

The boy's bed was quiet, a damp heat under the blankets.
The room in the backyard over the garage,
his own world. A drunken mother
asleep in the big house.

She only stayed because he told her to. Or because
it's different from being alone. But after, while he slept,
she couldn't move. As she walks
there's something she's not telling herself.
She's not allowing the words to form.

She's seen it.
How the tomcat bites the scruff

of the female's neck so she can't get away;
you can hear it hurting her and still she wants it.
The girl doesn't want it though. It's not that
she wants. She wants the part he keeps to himself,
what's back of those eyes.

He's hanging around the back door of the school.
She takes her time, sauntering down the hall,
switching her ass back and forth. She knows how to walk.
She saw him grinning at her after class.
He's there as she pushes the door open,
the orange sunset on his teeth, grinning.
He's smart, he's a fool, they all are.
She's had white boys before, but this one's different.
When he looks at you it's like a man looks at a woman,
        not at dirt.
There's that look of nothing to lose in his eyes, all surface.
Most white boys, you can see straight down inside them,
down to where they're afraid of you and it makes you want
to kick them,
kick them till they're out cold or at least not afraid anymore.
They think they can get it free. Well let them get it free
from their own kind.

High school. Those white girls
are a game too, they look at you
like you're some kind of bug,
something to get their white men to step on.
She just looks back at them
and turns her green eyes cold.
They can't take it. They look away.
They can't take much of anything.

Her friends, they're not much better.
Those soft black brown eyes
don't seem to want anything
except to keep from getting stepped on.
They keep to their own kind, where it's safe. She wants
something else. She wants

to kick the fuck out of something and get back
to the streets. There at least
they don't lie, don't promise anything.

That white boy, he doesn't promise anything either.
She wants him for the way he looks
at her breasts when they're in his hands, like he owned them.
That's the way he looks at the whole world
when he's walking down the street,
like he owns it but doesn't care.
She looks at him and wonders where in hell back down the line
she got those eyes that are like cold green water.
The two of them screw like they were crazy.
They each know more than anybody needs to know.
They don't need each other. They don't need anything.

COUNTY ROAD

The fog so close you can't see
two feet ahead, coasting with the
lights off anyway, no sound, not another car
anywhere, only the muffled sound
of your parents trying to tell you
it's reckless, the things you do. Coasting
the dark curves, patches of luminous fog
around scattered houselights, feeling your way.
That's how it is, always. Later you'll forget
how to live like this, they say.
Voices in your head. No way
will you forget. On the foggy road alone,
no sound of another car anywhere,
only the muffled city somewhere,
fifty thousand miles away, fifty thousand miles.

II

OLD

Along Claremont Avenue the stores are closing.
The streetlights have just remembered to come on, and the first
faint stars. In the pharmacy the old man
leans behind the counter in the middle of those
well-stocked shelves as it gets dark outside.
Only a few shapes cross the window. Now and again
a young face glances in with a look that says
old man you're past it, as if he were the enemy.
Across the street the bus stop with its huge old oak
that was here even before him.
The bench under it: he remembers being young there, with a girl.
No one sits there anymore, it's gone
ice-cold in the shadows, almost invisible.
The young kids waiting for the bus would rather stand
at the edge of the curb, under the streetlamp
as the cars go by. There's that look in their eyes.
They want to see who's in them.

LABOR

The streetcleaning machine chugs around a corner,
the asphalt in its wake black and wet.
The repair crew's been up since five;
this is the first break of the day.
The men lean against the big silent machines
sipping coffee from the take-out,
their yellow hard-hats overturned on the ground.
Little puffs of steam whisk away on the breeze.
Their strong hands wrap around the paper cups,
fingers crooked from handling so many tools,
from lying upside-down under cars,
from crawling into the ducts of houses,
from breaking up asphalt.
Only the young one in the plaid shirt
has smooth hands. He was hired last week
but already he knows how to whistle at a woman.
Soon he'll be a man.
Time to get back on the job –
there's nothing to whistle at this early in the morning anyway,
nothing walking down the street.

Farther down the street in the donut shop window:
rows of empty metal trays, and toward the back
a young woman dipping donuts in a vat
of chocolate, turning them quickly to dry on racks.
She doesn't even stop to lick her fingers.

The sun edges around buildings, spilling crates of shadow.
Daylight's better than the night. The far stars
are deceptive, like the diamond rings in their black velvet cases,
but the jewelry store window is bare now,
as if everything had been stolen.
At midday the shop girls will stop by on their lunch break

and stand at the glass trying to decide
which one they'd choose if they had the chance.

The corner coffeeshop opens at seven,
but nobody comes in till later, eight or so.
Only the workmen, but they don't come to sit.
They send one of the crew in to pick up the coffee.
The woman wipes her hands down her apron,
lights a cigarette. In the back her husband's still snoozing.
He said they'd buy a bigger place someday, but that
was ages ago, when they got married.
When you're young you'll say anything.

Back at the repair site they've started up the jackhammer.
It'll wake everybody up. The sound carries all down the street.
The young woman goes to the door to unlock the donut shop
and the day officially begins. At the coffeeshop
the woman blows out a sigh of smoke;
in awhile her husband will be awake.
The workmen are down in the ditch.
They don't look up
as sunlight crawls over the ragged edge of asphalt,
blazes on the dirt and warms their backs.
The first of the office workers have started filing down the
        sidewalk,
surprised that they're digging up the street again,
that so much labor's needed under there.

Most people move around from job to job.
They'd rather get paid for nothing.
Between times they sidle down the streets
stoned on whatever. It's the slow change of lighting
that turns afternoon to evening.
The young men stand around on the curb drinking beer,
muscles ruddy in the sunset light, careless
of cops cruising past, their women
hanging on their arms laughing
one notch too loudly as if deep down
they understood themselves.
These women, they used to be the wild ones,
they let themselves get passed around.
The ones who got pregnant
just disappeared.

The men will disappear too, one way or another.
But for now they stand there, cocky, with their arms crossed
and women hanging on them as if someday
they'd be millionaires. There are always
enough of them to line these streets,
drinking while the cool breezes come out of hiding,
bringing things back, making them remember
what they are, that they've got nothing. But that's more
than anyone likes to think about.
So somebody turns on a radio.
They lean back and let their bodies float
off a bit, just to lighten the load.
It takes only a few notes
to make a melody, the rest
is empty space. It's the time spent waiting
between jobs, between anything
and the next. It takes only a few notes
but you have to remember.
You have to remember
or it's lost.

Near where the freeway lifts
out of Oakland and into the bridge
to San Francisco
the apartment buildings are faded
1920s'.
Doug lives there.
The frustration.
Working in the Frosty Freeze on Broadway
and playing guitar in his room at night.
It tries to come out through the fingertips.
But the hands:
they're not good enough.
Everything stays inside.

That crazy lady lives nearby,
all day walking up and down
hunched under her umbrella
in a downpour only she can see.
And the black devil-man who cuts his hair
in the shape of two horns and flourishes his cape
when he says hi to Doug. He knows
exactly what he's doing, elegant, even
in this. He's no fool. He's found his niche.

Doug hasn't. He knows it.
He'd tell you everything if you'd listen,
but the words don't quite work either.

He likes to drive fast on the freeway, in control.
To feel the curves
accelerating through his arms under
slow-motion explosions of orange and magenta
fading to smoke as the lights spark on.
The night is clear and fresh, the hills
covered with lights that quiver

like raindrops on the windshield.
He's driving, just driving around.
Where to?

Doug's the kind of guy who says
he might make it someday
but doesn't believe his own words.
If he says he'd be happy to take you
anywhere you want to go, if only
he could come too,
would you go with him now?
He means:
how much have you ever loved anyone.

RAIN

The bay the color of steel, of a warship
with scattered sun and cloud on its flanks,
the color of a battlefield
after it's all over,
of a soldier's mind when there's nothing left to kill,
in the immediate vicinity anyway,
and he can rest
but what is that kind of rest worth?
There's always going to be something left alive.

The water from a tin cup
tastes thin and substanceless,
you can never get enough.
It's not that the first time wakens
a bloodthirst, it's that you cross over
to a country where everything's different,
a country of men
who don't know what they're after.
Everything tastes thin.
You take it all in, trying to get satisfied.
Then you just shut off.

Rain zig-zags down between the hills.
It shatters on rooves, and there are people inside
just sitting around listening.

If you're an ex-soldier you're out walking in the rain,
you're used to it. Hands in pockets,
the sidewalk full of shoes scraping past,
trousers, the bunched hems of dresses under coats.
You look at people from the bottom up.
Sometimes a pair of women's eyes catches
at your throat, at the way it was when you were a kid,

always wanting to know what came next,
like a movie full of possible surprise endings,
which way would it turn out?

But you never expected this. Never thought
the whole thing could just go on and on,
no end in sight, not much happening, just the rain,
the grey sidewalk and the shoes, soggy shoes
filled with other people's lives. The warm women
hurrying beneath their dresses.
Out on the street
you see people in-between things, never
the place they've left or where they're going, only
their faces with that look of expectation.

Except of course for the ones who live out on the street,
who stay there rain or shine, slumped in doorways,
sunk in their own eyes.

Further off the hills are blurred with white mist.
It's coming down hard there too. But from here
it just looks like a white mist that slowly blows and changes.

OAKLAND

A dead moon rises
over the California hills. It's bright
with second-hand light, something
you'd pick up in a Salvation Army store
and put down again.
The dead moon rises over Oakland
and the small-time burglars have something to see by,
something to lose, something to get caught in.
It rises beside the used bookstores, it looms
between office towers, it duplicates itself
in the windows of every tall building.
The bars are open; that's about all.
A drunk stumbles around the corner; in his mind
he's going around the corner of every city he's
ever lived in: what does it matter?
Sooner or later they all end up here
in this place which is many places:
all the strongest memories put together.
So that out of all the women
there is one woman, out of all the cities
one city, out of all the jobs
one job, twenty, thirty years of it,
and now he has a life, recognizable, a tale to tell.
And a friend or two: Frank becomes Jack becomes Bill.
It's okay, the friend doesn't know who he is anyway,
he's none the wiser. Sure they did all those things together.
They both admit it. They've known each other all their lives.

The women are out on the street all right, but you barely
          see them
unless you know what you're looking for. They lean in
          the shadows,
in the cracks of buildings, and then step into the light
as the men pass. They don't step out for the drunks though,

they just look at them, staring at that same drunk they've seen
stumbling down the streets of three different cities,
the same crooked body, the same red face.

Around one a.m. the people start pouring out of the movie
        theater.
In a few minutes they're gone. Crowds are like water.
Then it's just the street again.

After you've been on the street awhile
the moon is just one more thing out there.
The billboard says: Oakland Is Beautiful,
and it is. Somebody's shouting, but they always shut up.
A woman. A man. A glass broken.
You can see the wall where it smashes. A thousand walls,
they're all the same. Somebody's shouting, sometimes it goes on
and on. But eventually, one way or another,
they always shut up.

SPRING

The hills plunge through mist as if their contours
romped, but they're dead-still, made in those shapes
long ago. From early morning
the black and white cows have walked
straight through walls and columns of mist as if
their eyes could only see three feet in front of them anyway.

The hills in the morning: a green so delicate and wild
it almost shimmers backwards out of existence.
The cows stand sideways
on the hill gazing three feet in front of them
into empty air or they move in that slow
stumbling shuffle over the dirt clods. They could walk
straight through outer space not blinking an eye.

The fault opens up five feet wide in some places.
The small earthquake in the middle of the night:
the world swaying so hard it almost falls
out of orbit,
with only the sound of glasses
chattering in the cupboard.

Beside the run-off line: the skeleton
of one of last year's cows.
The other cows just walk around it
as if it weren't there.
Or maybe somewhere in those eyes
like bells too far away to hear
they already know.

At sunset the farmer
comes out of his white house on top of the hill
and watches his cows as if
he wished they belonged to him,

as if their four legs didn't move in their own time.
If they knew a little more
they could just walk off and leave him.

Always the hills and mist are making their mute gestures.
People get the feel of it, that's all they ever get.

The sheep stand around like errant clouds.
The lambs just sit in the grass, brand-new,
they haven't been here long enough to dirty their fur.
They rest awhile, looking around
as if they don't quite know how to behave.
Then they heave up on those scrawny legs
unfolded for the first time in the world.
And right away they get it:
the feel of being alive.
They want to romp
over every corner of those green hills.

Land is nothing unless it's good for grapes.
In the smoky breeze of evening,
on the bare round hills the staked vines
drip with dew and under the leaves
water aches in those cool clusters.
All that wine, you know where it goes:
to the cities.
When a man gets tight that's where he goes too.
He'll drive his truck hard down the highway:
if he goes fast at least it feels
like there's someplace to go, if he pushes
he might break through.
The moon is so still over the vineyards,
it never gets mad about anything.
What good are those damn grapes
gleaming like ice when what he really wants
is a woman? Whiskey would do. But the women,
the women. Most of the time they're invisible,
even when they're right there.
And a man needs a woman
to disappear into once in awhile, like a deep fog.
That's why late at night he'll drive
to the city just for some company. But the city:
here and there in a doorway an old drunk
lying in the dark like an untied shoelace.
The drunks, they might as well be stuffed with straw
the way they lie there, clothes too big for them,
practically falling off.
And in a corner restaurant the middle-aged men
still lucky enough to make a little money
so they can sit there all night instead of lying
in the street – the place is full of them,
there are never enough women to go around.
So they sit there

with that abused look on their faces.
They drink to become invisible.
And the man who drove in all night from the vineyards,
he's been walking
up and down the streets
but she isn't there, the one he wanted,
the one he imagined all that time tending the grapes.
Instead he walks into a room full of men
who've been drinking so long their eyes
have the sheen of grapes in the moonlight.
The dewy night collects against the windows.
He looks around, but they're all invisible to each other.
The young ones with the charged eyes,
they keep their backs to the corners,
twisting a glass in front of them. You can see
they still have something on their minds.
Between gulps they stare into the glass.
It has a lot to teach them.

You're sitting there drinking.
Big windows overlook the bay,
little chinks of light opening and closing
on the water, too quick to catch hold of.
It's one of the signs – a wallet stuffed full
with not just money but cards, things
with your name on them, an address.
One of the signs
that things are half over.
All around the room the sunset
glows in people's drinks; it lights up yours too.
Looking out at the bay
you can sit and smoke,
sort things out alone.
In the corner a woman's hair
shivers with chance sunlight as she laughs;
the man she's with – his eyes
keep flicking down to her sweater.
When people first meet
they smile a lot, testing.
But you have to meet first.
So things are half over, what of it?
Tiny rainbows on the walls
where the sun splits through the drinks.
On the bay the lights open and close,
too quick to catch.
It's like that, isn't it.
Everyone will go their way. Eventually
you'll go yours too,
step again over the threshold
of a wrong house, a mistaken address.
Then the meal eaten, hardly speaking.
Those kids – how could they ever have come from
nothing, from two bodies? Now things are half over
and it's like it never happened. And later

lying all night in the darkness
beside the real distance, a distance
like the long open ocean past San Francisco Bay
that you'd gladly dive in and swim except you know
it goes on forever, beyond
the endurance of the body.

IT'S NEVER ENOUGH

Something about the time of afternoon.
Sunlight singes the tall wisps of straw and somehow
nothing's worth doing except lying down and drowsing
in the warm dust, the mint and lemon smell
of eucalyptus. Quick little winds shiver through
the trees and are gone; they hint
at a storm that doesn't come, ever.
And the little earth-tremors that say: someday.

Calico hills. The huge circumference of shadow
around each tiny oak.
You can see perfectly, even at a distance,
the miniature of light and dark in the leaves,
you can see it
with your eyes closed. The dull buzz
of motorcycles cutting up and down the hills.
The buzzing goes round and round
all sunny afternoons like this,
and the interminable construction of houses:
the saws, the hammers clunking away at dead wood.

All the sounds are hollow, and they carry forever.
It's the sound of a crazy person butting his head against a wall.
The sound of a woman tapping fingers to a music
she's making up in her head and isn't telling.

Those bikers. I've seen first hand
how they smash into walls
and come out alive. Finding out
how far they can push those machines,
how much abuse they can take.
They want to see
if their bodies are any different from that,

if a life
is different from that. I know what they're after.

They'll push a woman into a corner where she can't
say no. Even though she knows
exactly what they're doing to her, and knows
they do it just because
they're careless, deliberate.
She's learned to need that violence, that searching,
even if it's secondhand. She needs to know
the world could blow up at a footfall; there's that danger
that makes it all worth something. And she needs them
to come back with that look in their eyes:
that insane sadness that can't be touched.

Something about the time of afternoon,
these bright, empty hills.
A biker shrieking around the short
hard curves like a penned-up goat
cracking his horns on the walls.

But all that is far away, a dull hollow buzz. The sun
sinks low and shows through the poison oak: emeralds and
        blood.
Afternoon's a good time for drowsing,
but evening won't be: the damp darkness in which
if you had a lover you'd take his hand and say:
let's go somewhere warm. But because you're alone
you'll have to remind yourself to get going.
So you close your eyes one more time to feel the sun
going down through the lids. It won't last long. It never does.

BALANCE

If you stand perfectly still and don't blink
you can see the horizon roll
against the rising moon. The motion's
just a little bumpy; if you don't blink you can see it.

People like to look up and see the moon.
They don't even know why they like it.
Their eyes are just pulled.

Sometimes a pair of lovers kiss in the night grass.
And then one of them, the man, catches it
nudging around a tree: the huge face
of everything he doesn't know,
a face full of blood. But more than that:
the thing is so distant he knows
he'll never know it, never get anywhere close.
There's nothing like that face
to make him pull nearer to the girl, but also
it makes him want to look away.

What's a man to do with his own insides?
How can he reconcile
the girl and this moon,
how can he put a world together?

The girl is angry when he gets like this.
After all, she wants
what she wants. All men are drifters.
They're like seeds of milkweed.
The slightest wind can push them
in the wrong direction and then they root there.

A woman, she has the hard job.
Once she finally has a family
she has to watch them all, even her husband.
She has to herd them here and there making sure

they stay together. Any one of them could drift off.
Except the girls. They can handle
more than a man. Their feet are full of lead.
Somehow they know how to look at the moon
and still stay put.

Only once, the lovers were lying in the grass,
they were feeling loose that night and she got on top.
Then, in the middle of everything,
she accidentally looked up.
And she saw it too.

III

COLOR OF STARS

for Steve Schwartz

Rain comes down, mother-of-pearl, the freeway bent
into fog, its other end lost in angles downtown.
All this in your eyes: the reflections.
We watched that sunset together: magenta flares
over the black buildings, that moment
already changing into something it wasn't.
What about this thing we piece together then,
out of all that happens to us,
the story we come up with,
this life?

The brilliant green hills are turning grey, facing
toward night. Everyone keeps a few
backward places in their life that they look to
as little edens, before it all started. Places
where they made the wrong decision on purpose
so they can't return. Making that choice
because they'd rather kill a thing prematurely
than watch it die gradually by its own hand.

So we drive into these hills for the nth time,
the city lights buoyed up in blackness,
and try for the few words that will explain it.
The wind feels the same
as it always did, back at the beginning,
back when the whole world was going forward
with the force of a tide that only comes in, that wind
still going through our lungs.

Look up at those three stars.
Tell me.
Are there any words for what color they are.

Through the rows of glasses a forsaken
streak of light, as on the solitary spoons
the gleaming strokes –
when sisters and brothers meet
in a dark bar at ten in the
morning after many years,
when the initiates of a family come together in the extreme
obscurity of their likenesses,
the closest friends
become bystanders.
The distances we've just come
to be together
would have taken some explorer's lifetime.

Irish coffees at ten in the morning:
cool rind of cream on the lip and the bitter whiskey beneath
whatever we talk about.
Whatever our friends fell in love with in each of us alone
is fraudulent. Whenever we're together it seems
there's an eye loose here, a gesture there, and out of every
        sentence
one syllable we all pronounce the same. As though between us
there is only one
child of our parents, whom we haunt and share.

There are sea anemones that by touch distinguish their own
from the others, and carefully do away
with the others.
There are single cells that choose to live in one
undulating raft
to navigate, synchronously, the waves.

All day we walk among the shops with their identical items.
And stand looking a long time
at what we know by heart.
The Golden Gate in fog.

The Golden Gate in sunshine
the color of rust, not golden at all.
Of all who jumped or meant to jump,
of all who meant to drown,
most leapt toward the harbor,
the city in their eyes.
Along the dock supports at waterline,
half in half out, the large pink starfish
neither crawling up
nor letting go. Just grasping.
Large pink hands which are nobody's.

On the hundred hills
the straw signals in the wind.
Sometimes a whole arc of it shines.

Every family is different, but in each one
they have the same eyes.
Every time they look at one another
there's that mirror.
There's no help for it.

Our family's eyes are the color of mud,
of cliffs, full
of tiny landslides that amount to nothing.
They are the sheen on puddles,
the sun that doesn't see anything better to light up.

Of my two brothers the older is always watching
the younger, and the younger is always going somewhere.
Or he used to be; right now
he's flying us in circles over the hills
where we all grew up. That small cross of shadow
is us, twisting into a bird, a straight line.

Families are all the same. They talk to one another
inside their heads, thinking the others can hear.

The sunset flashes on our faces as we twist away
over the shoreline, over the pale red foam,
but our tiny shadow stays back in the hills, rumpling over them,
over that spot we all know. Long ago
each of us fell and hurt himself
one too many times and opened those eyes
that could have been any one of ours

to his own face reflected in the dirt.

North Berkeley at night perfumed
by a thousand gardens.

Further off the eucalyptus trees
clatter in the wind like runaway herds,
the hills dark and empty as caves.

Who knows why/anyone leaves the place
they were born? The wind in the trees
pulled through a hole in the heart.

Out of the ice cream parlor
people come two by two,
sharing a taste, walking off
with their arms around one another.
The liquor store's shut tight; bottles glint on the shelves,
a sliver of streetlight in them.
The post office: ghost-town in red, white and blue.
A couple of teenagers lean against it in the shadows,
their radio turned up loud. The music – it's all the same –
the sound of watching everything from a car window
and letting it all flow out of reach.

The North Berkeley houses sit quiet,
all their lights damped out, waiting
for the wind to lift them.

Who knows why anyone comes back
to the place they were born.
That restlessness in the trees again, the sudden gust
that rushes to the brain like blood. It's as if
you'd never left but dozed off
and in the dream believed you could have been
someone else for a moment, in a far place.
The teenagers lean in the shadows and listen
to the music. It's always moving.

Piled into any old clunker we could all fit in,
eight or ten of us,
whoever composed a momentary spasm of the group,
and rode it like a kingsize bed down the jetstream highway.
Past sunset and on into dusk,
the odd shared landmark posting the way,
and then the car left behind, gleaming on an angle.
Stony disfigured hill,
the guardianship of a few cattle we had to pass, magnified
through the lens of their intent, icy heartshaped heads
at home in those ambling machinations of bones
whose shapes are safe and hidden, just below the skin.
Arched paralyzed oaks, bright
bright stars on that long-legged hunch uphill to the hotsprings.
We were each other's
lost tribe,
clandestine,
incestuous,
one at a time floating backwards on the hotpool below
        frozen oaks,
guided underneath by the others' fingers, and balanced
between augury and trust,
one at a time became guiltless,
a guest of strong starlight,
hills that surrounded yet took nothing from us.
Though unclothed in that nearness,
the nearness of everything it seemed,
we could not have told you – parents, interrogators –
one word of it. Beside ourselves in firelight,
foreshortened in sleep,
falling all night long for the mind's mimicry of events.
For in your language we could not breathe.

BY FLASHLIGHT

Camped out here once, much younger,
with Paul – his muscles all awake beneath the shirt –
whom none of us would touch. Betsy, Jan, and I
lying wide apart in the clearing
like freshly branded cattle,
wet grass at the edges of our eyes.
The icy heat, the paralysis, the wish . . .

the stars so far apart up there
you could see between them

but trusted ourselves even less
and so lay there
knowing only what we felt:
those who ministered to "the real world"
were full of empty threats.

The firs jut three feet farther
into the sky-map now.
The flashlight leads us back,
you, my favorite remembered friends: for this we need
one set of legs to share, my eyes, and the flashlight,
grazing frictionless over the ground, as guide.

For my part, I come back
every few years to take a turn through these woods,
our piece of luck for a summer, eight acres
of redwood and huckleberry,
papery skulls embedded in the forest floor, the bulkier bones
we could never assemble: of deer, or stray cattle, or some other
        animal
we never saw alive.
Which of you keeps up the breadbaking, in memory

of that first laughable sunken loaf? Which of you
still moons at fourteen-year-old boys for us all?

Sitting by the fire, muscles tired
from carrying all three of us around.
Funny how little I've learned, when everyone else
has grown taller around me, like the fir trees,
shutting out a little more light.
The taste of coffee, deep at night, when nobody could care.
The bat that sweeps at eye-level through the twilit house.
The hidden inhabitants, the unknown guests.
Huge forests, fostered on neglect.
The sensuous probing spiders.
Lights that get left on all night.
The sudden attack of rain on the roof, any time.

BAY LAURELS

for Steve Schwartz

The canyons come to me this time
by way of a letter,
folded around bay leaves picked in that place overlooking
the continuous sunlit hills,
the army base at its distance,
and the filmy wandering blue of the bay,
that single noncommital edge.
I've been gone seven years now.
My body must have renewed itself
once in that time, replacing cell by cell so as not to lose
the overall structure.
You've sent the bay leaves as promised, meaning: memory.

The laurels engaged in shadowplay on the ground
where we sat putting things together, as friends can,
who come together so rarely.
All the years of your restlessness.
You belonged to the spirit that was leaving
the country then, leaving
but never for good.
Just one of the ways we've changed places without meaning to.
Even the stamps on our letters: we've begun
to speak with objects, as citizens of places do.
Yours, flat blue and bright
shadowless yellow toward which an unmanned
probe falls, "Understanding the Sun."
Mine, a fleshy romantic rose, focussed
with tiny spheres of dew,

shade-green leaves
spiralling up from blackness. "La Rose Montréal." We've been
apart too long.

More, I notice myself undergoing strange, unkind thoughts.
        Perhaps
a subtle tampering goes on in the cells after all.
That bare wire in the brain, like touching something cold: *ah yes,*
he's not here, the one you want in certain moments,
when no one else is right.
Those overexposed canyons
of bay laurels where the leaves come from. Until you sent them
I never put together their sweet, smoky smell
with the hills that bore so much walking, it was just
the way those years smelled.

Old shoes,
where are you taking me now?
You who've spent a night in the Pacific
farther out than I dared to go –
and I found you again, bedraggled in the morning,
separated from each other by fifty feet of beach,
salt in all your seams, and sand, and seaweed.
That time I thought you were lost for good.
Old shoes, the first my grown feet accepted
without the deep ache that comes
of trying on what others have meant for me. Don't worry,
it's me they're laughing at, those who find us unfashionable.
Our last day upright on the earth
we'll fit each other still.
Don't let them trick you into sorrow.
If they stow you in a box that's too small
in the depths of some unfamiliar closet, remember
the walks we took, the close
companionship of shoes and feet.
Remember the long
mouthwatering days, each place
we rested, just taking it in. We took it in
for a reason, for the time when they'll stow us away
where there is nothing to see, to do, to feel.
And when you've relived it all as much as you need,
when you tire of standing still,
remember the imperceptible holes, how they tore and grew,
the socks, pair by pair, those soft
kittens that came between us, playful, how soon
the walking wore them down.

THE PHOTOGRAPH

for Steve Schwartz

The last carlights are making their way along the edge of
      California hills,
one pair heading one way, another the other,
and the first big planet is beaming
beautiful coded lights at us, variations on a theme
in darkness.
The hills have never been so black.
The car heading toward us enlarges like a dying star
about to vanish and take as much of the world with it.
The other a lava-flow down the hill, fiery red.
Without that small single oak, plateaued by wind, at the edge of
      vision,
the one you planted there with your fine sight,
the one you took care, by accident, to include,
the absolute length of this moment would have fooled us.
I know what the fog protects
down there, between the hills.
Places I've walked, dusty gullies
that floated all manner of things away, in summer.
Places that never existed, apart from us,
though anyone looking
can see the backdrops.
Oakland spread out like an engine, disassembled, in the afternoon
      haze.
San Francisco lit up each night like a control panel,
as if something huge and godlike were about to come in for a
      landing.

The carlights are making their last stab into darkness.
Fog, surf.
Yes. To talk to you is always to touch home.
How like you, to leave that oak, just at the edge.
Your hand in the world.

And every night the same stars keep coming back without warning.
Not one of them I can see with my eyes in my lifetime has left.
So. This is a photograph of time in the place we grew up.
Time, which fools us
with moments. Moments that don't exist,
apart from us.

FOLKLORE

Where there is injury, pardon.
Where there is darkness – darkness.

I

Those nights. They came after days during which my father's cigarette glowed like a rose caught in sunset on a distant hillside. Then he would stub it out and night would fall.

The air would be traversed by strange scents emanating from night-blooms, and the passion vine broadcast for miles around its coded message, wound along the trellis. The fruit dangled, frosted with silver and fur, and inside: a smile of translucent teeth, a mouth full of smuggled jewels. The honeysuckle threaded everything with white and yellow trumpets, evaporating in a sweet gas. So sweet that one inhalation inflames the nostrils and after that is no longer detected.

All night long my parents slept, breathing it, my mother facing that darkened place she would always roll toward, the open window to the wild hill. And my father next to her under the light, fallen asleep in the middle of himself as in a field he'd been crossing, the book still open beneath his fingers, and the circling moths, with wings of powdered lead, whirling shadows around his face.

The pepper tree was like a sunset against the blue summer sky. A pink hail littered the grass. All summer I'd watch, but there were no black peppercorns. It never turned to something I understood. That was back when there was just one word for each object.

Translucent rains moved from tree to tree, focussing on one at a time, a lens. A shrub whose name I could never remember because it didn't suit it, leafless until summer, in spring was fashioned of flowers so minute they had to be brought right up to the eye: sprays of pink froth, a fountain out of the ground. Rain slid into the seams of the magnolias, those echo-chambers of ivory. In the morning you could pick up a fallen petal and drink a raw perfume.

The street I knew, with its black nights and streetlamps that shone on the magnolias, magnolias that were like wilder streetlamps.

But up near the almond tree, back of the house, was a whole hill of quiet that couldn't be grasped. Mornings I'd wake to the hammering of houses being built, but it was the woodpecker in the almond tree, riddling it with even holes, round and round the trunk. Signalling the end of spring the almond would let down its blossoms, frail and fragrant. Later the fuzzy green summer fruit would come. One after another I'd crack them open, looking for the almond, the thing I knew as an almond, finding only a tasteless amber jelly, that rubbery sac of bitter milk.

It was the almond tree that drew me on the first sad day of my life. It was the morning you could see in my brother's face the first thing he'd lost. For hours he stayed in his closed room with the empty bird cage, its queer little door open.

Some days my brother would play his flute. Even practicing scales the notes were burdened with winds that blew through landscapes made visible by his playing. He would hold it in a fine straight line from his lips to his ear, listening deftly, mimicking water-drops that trickled in the highest, secret mountains, finding our thirst.

Fireflies. But no, they are houselights scattered through the ever-greens. The garden is an orchestra of silent instruments the musicians left behind, still lying in their positions, not a sound left in them. The wind's arms rise with a huge generosity, a conductor's arms, and then, inexplicably, lose heart.

Far off in the woods the white spots have fallen from the flanks of the young stags. Their fuzzy horns, still unprotected, nick the low-hung branches. They aren't used to it yet, this crown, these new probes, like the penis of an eleven-year-old boy who lies awake tonight for the first time.

No matter how many nights these boys lie alone on the rough sheets, they still won't know why autumn will come, altering everything, bringing amnesia of the little they've understood, listening dumbly, happily, to the crickets, the sleighbells of summer.

Persuaded by my mother's expertise in the secret and sometimes occult behavior of the natural world, the night we were called up to witness the night-blooming Cereus, the flashlight in my father's hand, its beam leading somewhere into the ground, while privately my brother whispered: Cereus is a star.

Older brothers are gifted with natural military minds. A nimbleness, casual abilities in sleights of hand and eye. Conducting with suave nonchalance experiments in which small animals and little sisters serve interchangeably as prey and pupil, experiments devised not so much from ill-will as to delineate a testing ground, a sort of school in which my attendance was mandatory and from which it was unlikely I would ever graduate. These minor tyrannies could be counted on to deflect me from the truth of any situation. Snails. Slugs. A beetle that struck between the shoulderblades as I ran away.

Every boy carried, in some back pocket of memory, scale maps of the neighborhood containing secret and strategic locations. Tree forts, lean-to's, natural rock caves, even holes in the ground. That last summer before the forced exile into adolescence, beneath the acacia tree my brother and his friend would dig a huge pit, watched constantly by the cats, their slit pupils evolved perfectly for peering at a distance through the long grass. Being younger and less able to keep out of harm's way, I would be ordered to scrape with bare fingernails all the dirt from the dirt floor of the fort.

Whether the night-blooming Cereus bloomed or grew shy in the presence of the flashlight, I don't remember. Gullibility has its dignity. And optimism, eyes. A refusal to be domineered by mistrust. If my eyes were on the sky at the wrong moment, praise misdirection, which promises the longer more adventurous road. It's true enough that stars are flowers blooming only in darkness. Praise the moment, if from that moment on I was lost to the rest of them, one hand still holding a fold of mother's hem, while the shadowy cats tightrope-walked along the trellis, mingling with stars and fruit, the slim grenades of the passion vine. Imagination on its tether, I was up there with the cats, who prefer to encircle any event from above, defining its borders like gods.

Under the acacia lit with yellow pollen, beneath the pines where the straw sprays out in a structure of crystals, startled from cool caverns of dirt, the insects labored, falling over crumbs. In those hours between two and five p.m. it doesn't matter which shady tree you drag your body under, the mind goes walking, slowly, with no relief. Ants, building with crumbs. And sowbugs that play dead in your hand, sequestered, curled into hollow grey balls. Potato bugs climb over the exposed roots, their unwieldy heads burned out and blind. Over the ground the shadows sway, in and out of focus. And afternoon registers, incandescent, along the street of sycamores, whose bark comes free in puzzle-pieces, leaving a raw geography of the world.

    Someone must know how the house fits into the street, the street into a map of the world. But nothing that happens inside this house will be recalled, nothing will escape into history. Outside, the night like a developing photograph, moon and stars, the bamboo shaking its paper knives. And how far out of hearing the upstairs windowlight. How far. How grave.

Not only the night-blooming Cereus. The intimacy of all living things, especially those that blossom. Any given spare moment we'd hear the chirping of shears, and she'd be out in the garden. Grasping, letting fall. The same precision, the same care with which, the rest of the week, she performed early-morning surgery, routine examinations on pregnant women.

Strange relations, by proxy. Forbidden knowledge we merely overheard but had no right to reply to or repeat. Diseases. Case histories. Half my childhood friends born in my mother's hands.

Her weakness: loud tropical flowers. Their clairvoyance for storm, generating overgrowth: that something might survive. Tent-like shaggy leaves of the banana tree, its rare bursts of fruit splayed out red from the trunk like hands which withered without reaching their true shapes. A dozen kinds of orchids climbed and grew pristine, their flat, painted faces enduring the cold rains. Whole continents sprang alive in her garden, ignorant of their origins. The fishpond my father built for her, rock-rimmed, as if a giant had stepped through, leaving a footprint which had immediately filled with waterlilies, papyrus, all the floral props of ancient civilizations. These are the books she'd read in bed, surveying from her high lit window the plot of history, the layered sediment of explicable event. What she relied on to have deposited her safely. Here. Small black print on an illumined page.

One year a single freak frost took from her half the orchids, the banana, the night-blooming Cereus.

A two-year drought and then they were gone: the papyrus, the passion vine, all that remained of her imported world.

Around this time she began to snore, as if to express a satisfaction with sleep, or else a deepening reluctance to return to us. Or perhaps simply to keep my father company in that sound, his sound, which seemed to extend far beyond the room and to explicate his dreams in unknown tongues to the listener.

My father asleep inside a book, my mother among those loud tropicals which blossom. Continents without origin. Diseases without cure. Grasping, letting fall. The withering and the thriving, all at once.

Purple, papery, wisteria wreathed the house, and each May a white box would arrive, its lid lifting to release not music but the smell of gardenias, their number compounded by one. What defines the union this gift symbolized, my father to my mother, if one who came of it may speak for it? But I can't. In the end we carry forward only a little of each story.

In the evenings white ginger stood exalted in its leaves, anticipating stars, each point of origin, each needle in a nerve. Always the freedom, always the need, unresolved.

Whatever came or is yet to come is of this middle realm, for which the human eye is the inevitable instrument. Awe and disappointment, unique and to scale. Out of bounds the uninhabitable regions, both larger and smaller, in which all of this lies innocently hidden. Just as here among us go unnoticed those merry-go-rounds whose horses appear or reappear, ghostwise, in the fuchsia leaves.

In the evening air: purple bells made of satin, ladies in violet ball-gowns. The unopened ones hang like cocoons, slit, a startled magenta creature inside.

From the raw shoots, pale and striated, odors rise up in flames. And the stars freshly awake in the green dusk: crumbs of fire.

There is a terror at happiness, at feeling your own steps, one after another, like minor earthquakes. It's after the uproar of spring, when the sky unrolls those roads into blueness and quiet, that the clouds begin to shuttle through, carrying their cargo.

A paper kite, mauve in the light that has already forgotten us, still tugs at its string, attached to the earth somewhere.

This is when it is first detected, not as a thought, but because of the surprise. When the smell of the fuchsias comes tolling.

When we were young and all living in the same house, before any of us knew to imagine ourselves elsewhere, my sister on piano, my brother with his flute, in separate rooms, diagonal, the whole house between them, filling it with noise. Under her fingers the keys became a charging army. The flute meanwhile subtle, countering. A city of chimneys sprouting smoke in the rain. The lush rubbery garden afterwards, the quivering egg that broke from each leaf. Whatever is locked up in the wise bark of the trees. Whatever the memory is still convinced of. The woodsprite with pale yellow hair still lives invisibly beneath the pomegranate bush, where I left her, in the other world.

Like a cool tub it sat there, in the middle of the night, striped green and silver, hovering on its curved edge. All summer it occupied that spot. When one watermelon was finished, another would be there. Like all things of which there must be unequal portions, it tormented my sister; this was the summer of her turning fourteen. One night, the house asleep, she crept downstairs in her long flounced nightgown and dug the whole heart out. Bite by bite, icy and red beneath the kitchen window.

It's true no one was looking, but I am looking now and in some ways it is still then. Because of the years between us there is a gap, like that between the first up the mountain and the last, though a rope binds them together.

There is a way in which a single act becomes a legend, the way a child's first mispronunciation of a word becomes a family's intimacy, referencing that one instant forever. Morning swelled, gold sparks drifted through the kitchen, settling over everything, the watermelon and its cold oval shadow. The silt of summer.

For the last weeks the daylight hours have fallen short and shorter. Transfixed by yellow porchlight to a wicked chartreuse, shadow-plants spring up all around. Enamel primroses, and snowdrops looking down like tiny streetlamps from their tall stems. The garden bears its losses with a quiet we have never accustomed ourselves to: even the crickets have taken their gypsy music elsewhere.

The little St. Francis looks out from his jagged pulpit high on the cedar trunk, clay birds landing on his clay shoulders. He'd be lost without them, for they were born that way, joined. Like all saints he gazes straight ahead at a single point. The black veils of the cedar boughs shade him, for he is frail, and they live here.

As the youngest, I remember when my father and brothers used to work outdoors. They'd go halfway around the house just to douse the crooked ring of cedars under St. Francis with their urine. Standing beside one another or alone they seemed distanced, as if in some animistic prayer.

But I remember St. Francis most for those April dawns when I was the first awake. The amaryllis siphoned its pinkness from underground springs of cologne. The sun would just touch him and he'd blush as if a woman had come too near, and all day the jays would land and take off again, taunting him like delinquent boys, for he was no bigger than they were.

Boidae had all the illustrious markings of her species. Her back zig-
zagged with a bolt of brown lightning, she could have slid through
the grasses with the lesser snakes, that emblem on her back, and
been queen. But she was my father's snake and would blandly curve
around his shoulders, push her blunt prehistoric head along his
cheek, up through the frames of his glasses, and emerge looking out
from his forehead as if he were some strange rock. My father would
let her go as she willed, looping about his neck, he with a playful
look on his face that hid a private dare he'd made, something he
wouldn't share with anyone.

When Boidae was young, only a foot long, he'd coil her up like
a length of live wire and stuff her in a pocket along with his stetho-
scope, to startle the nurses. He delighted in carrying live things
around, pretending they just happened to be there. Sometimes he'd
pick a fresh wet flower to lay at my mother's place at the table.

But it's not easy to tell if a snake is happy or sad.

Now the cat likes to follow my father around, and my father
follows him. They seem always a little lonely for each other.

We each leaned, palm down, with all our weight, into the fresh con-
crete and then it rained, and the handprints in sunken relief turned
silver.

Present at this ceremony of hands:

our mother;

our father;

the elder of my two brothers, the faint smile and beard already
putting him just beyond reach;

my sister, with the beautiful half-formed breasts;

and next to me my other brother, the one we would each in turn
admire;

while the handprints, orderly, grew smaller. Mine the last.

We're born into the family in a kind of sleep, chaotic, unmem-
orable . . . the awakening occurs much later. This archive began not
in words, on a day whose details don't matter. Only the handprints
remain, confirming as if by chance an earlier existence, beside the
bird of paradise inflamed in the twilight, orange and blue.

On awakening though: to be true to that first glimpse! – that
was the vow. Never to betray.

And from that moment on I have memories.

Huge walls of estates torched with flaming bougainvillaea, nearly sunset. Illusory fire of the tropics, purple, orange, magenta flowers. The memory makes fiction of us all, blazing and changed. Grandmother teaching music in China, long ago. And Aunt Jo, the one friend who came forward with her out of that time like a held breath, into the moving world. Orchids, seascapes. The perfume in a shell. Grandmother, up and down the scales, trying to decide whether or not to marry our eventual grandfather back in America. There are relics of this era: two royal chairs carved in the Chinese cloud pattern, each with an inset oval marble backrest, one saying: restless seascape, the other: mountain. Aunt Jo, fictional aunt. My mother named for her.

A coconut palm arcs over the surf, coconuts bowled in and out with the waves, my brother up the trunk already, hugging and leaning away. Then stays perched awhile, having cut down a monstrous smooth green fruit for us, his usual distance from the family.

Green on blue, unreal atlas of islands – plumeria, frangipani, unpronounceable flowers and stranger fruit, odd umbilical modes of growth. Six kinds of banana, each with the flavor or texture of some other fruit. Unpredictable manifestations. Tropical offspring. The three older kids on ti leaves tobogganing down steep jungle slopes.

The sun goes off like a flashbulb as the day's images disintegrate slowly and forever on the etched photographic plate of a four-year-old brain. No twilight this far from home.

After dark insects parade, bright as cartoons in the grass, spotlit beneath windows. Costumed and exotic as the Vogue models that parade between mother's searching flipping hands as she sits in those windows in the tropical night. Hardly women anymore. Subliminal faces windblown, immobile on the page. Among all the faces of the family, the one my mother most resembles, her own mother's best friend.

All day the blue geometries of waves charge and pass intact through one another, perturbing ripples, lines that don't die out.

Lines of convergence. Wading into the waves, mother's hand like an udder, her large guarding body. And then that strange embrace beginning, just underwater, time speeding down. Me carried off screaming, branded with an illusory fire that would not fade, the three older kids closing in with handfuls of sand toward the beached jellyfish like an open eye.

One more memory: charred volcanic seascapes, the brittle foam of those mountains. Where the ocean wears at it, black stretches of negative sand. No longer mother's side of the family, with its tropical incarnations. My father's side. The grey recurrent dream of eastern Europe. His father taking off with a best friend at age fourteen, first for England, then the U.S., where later my father would spend his childhood peering down into the La Brea's black claustrophobic prehistory. Those cumbersome creatures, in their last moments, mired like flies.

Formal monuments.

My father was given no middle name, just an initial, J., like a password.

J. for the best friend. Secret names. The ones who escape.

II

At night the earth takes its place among the planets. The daffodils dim to the ghost of yellow, but their oniony smell seems to color the stars. Stars of scorched ice higher than cathedral windows. In the streets the dogs move like space-walkers over a dead planet, sniffing, remeasuring everything by smell, dispossessed. In daylight they'd wag their tails up and down the block without a thought. But dogs' ideas are close to the surfaces of their skulls: they sense the strangeness but can't act it out except by sitting at attention in the dim street, their long black shadows sunk into it, the eye of a needle.

A pond on a spring night becomes a musical instrument. Now and then the plucking of the water, where something of its own volition startles, and a cascade of droplets picks out the notes. Just there the pond lies, rimmed with mud, but the narcissus droop their star-shaped heads at the ground, exiled by inches. Exiled and un-mirrored.

BEAUTY

On these leaden days of early spring even one stray tentacle of sha-
dowy sun makes the ground steam. There is a slate-green dust which
frosts the backsides of certain trees, away from the wind, which
three young girls have just discovered. They go from trunk to trunk
finding the brighter shades, streaking it above their eyes, posing for
one another. A few of last summer's blackberries are left hanging
like lanterns in a storm of brambles, too deep for the birds and too
high for things that crawl the ground at night. Still the half-
fermented juice is good for staining the lips. The girls are just learn-
ing about beauty.

One day they'll be shown what their own beauty or lack of it
will do to them. Not one day, but many nights, nights they'll lie
alone sifting through incidents, certain instances which are the only
analogue of those steeply lengthening bones, the breasts filling
calmly, immutably as lakes taking in all that stormy and random
rain.

Quivering manzanita, alive with silver rain, a tree of ball bearings!
They go scattering, bouncing, as the birds lunge and recover and
fences cross, recross the county, stilled woodgrain whorling like
spring creeks. Back of the house, over the septic tank, on high crisp
stems the lilies have risen, a whole monastery of them, cowls faintly
aglow in the treeshade. The clouds, the little ones, won't say where
they're going, just that they're playing up there, they'll never tire.
Spring: so casual. A clump of ferns sticking up like the necks of
buried violins. As if we were the ones who were off elsewhere, all
those lost months, degraded by sorrow, in selfmade darkness and
rain.

We were gathering wild plums. Reaching for them, laughing, pelting one another with the little hard ones, then suckling at a juice so tart the tongue invents instant sweetness in its wake. Then touching lips, a breath caught in our mouths, from the future.

Cold purple shadows, and arrowheads of sunlight darting among the leaves, hypnotic – were we waking? or drifting off – transported, transposed to a greying place with its duplicate plum tree, plum pits scattered on the ground, closed eyelids pecked by birds . . . and we must have slept. Slept as if twisted in some violent death, eyes taped open to our own beginnings and endings, closed to the outside. The birds reaped the latitudes and longitudes with their flight, and then, isolated lightning, an old wound. And we felt our bodies flashing, dead for so long, phantom bodies flashing like lightning in the ground –

Thoughtless. We're thoughtless as June moving in and out of cloud, foolishly gathering up our things because who wants to spend the night beneath a plum tree, shivering. Those dreams, so far from here, just under the skin. Heading home with baskets quarried all afternoon, a bit off-balance, for we've been tree-drifting, unused to having legs. Now and again turning around for a look, the treetops glinting from a distance, brown, seeming to grow a quiet magnitude of plums hidden all afternoon as we perched on the branches, each behind its leaf just above us. The ones the trees were holding back, saving for their friends, the birds.

BEFORE THE FIRST BIRD THINKS TO BEAR
ITS WEIGHT FROM THE BRANCH

Each day before dawn comes a false dawn. It fools even the birds. They come flying, still asleep, to take up their places along the phone lines and relieve them of that unresolved talk. Such chaotic chirping! And then, sleep-flying back to their branches, falling silent for another four hours.

Cobwebs caught in the bushes: grandiose ruins of an obscure architecture. Meadow mists, siphoned and beckoned out of earth and air, blown and meandered. A lone spider, severed hand of winter, stringing up yet another grand, withering snowflake. But the thing I meant to show you, what this little walk through the woods is for: see it, under that bush. Still lying there, new to death, giving off a faint negative charge. Look how the wind flickers its fur in a parody of running. How wind enters its mouth, but not as breath. And the eyes, gelled in a line of sight snapped sideways, invisible as the beam of a flashlight left on at dawn.

The wind keeps coming from different sides as if, not the wind, but the directions themselves were changing. I needed to show you this. Maybe you'll explain what it means to tell us, lying there like that, after whatever took place in the dark. Lying on the loosely braided needles, the little silver roses fallen from the pines. In the off-light before sunrise, before the first bird thinks to bear its weight from the branch.

A light twinkling rain and the wild vines send their runners deep into the fields. Wherever they stop, the fruiting begins. Splash of waxy leaves, the mingling and the sowing, the way rooted things look into the future. Sunlight sheds its gentle ruinous warmth. The honeysuckle milked by bees, slowly, with dangling feet. The pollen rubbed from the open rose. And suddenly those summer mansions the wild vines built, with high blossoming walls, all have crumbled. A hummingbird comes haunting the invisible flowers.

Single hummingbird, dry breath buzzing in its wings, harmonica with no wind left. The fuchsias fallen. And wild cathedral rainy bells beginning, leaf plastered to leaf and hugging drunk in the first full storm. A few unclaimed fruits hang in their glory among the darkened boughs, wild grapes clouded with seeds, not even foreknowledge exactly, seeds meant to be stolen by birds. In the lilting translucent rain. Beneath magnanimous branches.

One day we went wading up the river, my aunt, my mother, and I. Stripped to our underclothes, our bottoms like balloons floating along the surface, the river wide and dusty, a green glass whose edges riffled among debris and weeds. Most of an afternoon we spent wading away from our clothes, while the water gave without a brain, caressing and inanimate, and our feet never quite touched ground, billowing along in soft river silt.

The sky of that day does not fade, blue and matter-of-fact as any day in summer, with the high migration of clouds, as always, restless for the ocean. When at last the sun squinting through the underbrush began to divide each rock from its shadow, we too could see that our own shadows had come for us. We turned around and made our way out of the river then, dripping, back to the bank where we began.

As we dressed I grew awkward, tripping over nothing. Already the crickets and the frogs had begun their nightly lessons, practicing out loud, and painlessly. That day my mother and aunt had been as sisters again, while I trailed along behind, more of a ghost, or a wandering bit of my father, so that pulling on the cold clothes again was like tugging twelve times, twelve times on the bell-rope which signals the end of one more day of happiness.

It is said the garden dreams during the day. When the light is brightest, green things turn inward, they sleep. And it must be true. For all during the dark, the wind couriers between trees. First one rustles, then another. Messages are borne many hundreds of miles in this way unimpeded.

Whether pine is understood by the cypress isn't known. Or oak by cedar, elm by sycamore. Yet bark may dilate or buds seize up in accordance with auguries concerning insects or weather. Each tree prepares itself by waking the others.

The branches hold ultra-still until we've passed safely under them, for ineptitude is dangerous, though sometimes, from excitement, they quiver. But not because of us! They are intercepting knowledge. That sweet heady smell is no smell at all. And imagine us thinking we have the nose for it.

A fine perspiration falls from the trees at the height of summer after weeks of no rain. If you sit near them with the wind blowing your way, every few seconds you'll be pinpricked with dew.

Tonight, a Thursday night, there is a comet scheduled to pass close to the world, showering down meteors. And everyone, with upended faces, is reminded of Gilles Villeneuve, the race car driver thrown from his car, who, in these few airborne moments, is replaced with even faster, riskier thoughts.

If you sit still long enough, through an entire summer, eventually the fine flowers of the eugenia will somersault, daubed with pollen, into your coffee or your wine, depending upon the hour of day. And the human clockwork, then, tending toward a fateful accuracy, will force you to rise and go indoors, to reappear only when it is once again time to strike the pose and the hour.

Fathoms down through the trees, those men who appear on fall mornings to build and rebuild the world of streets and houses, those strangers in workgloves: if they had looked up, how easily they could have seen. My sister standing on the fallen nightgown letting the sun touch her breasts through the window. Wanting to be seen – or just to be warm. It was the year our difference in age set us in exact proportion to each other.

The soft blur of notes near middle C, the swaying afternoon full of bees that lived in her throat as she read me stories. Saturday nights when she'd let me dress her, a huge beautiful doll twice my size. She and her best friend in the bathroom light as they made themselves up: their mirrored eyes like the dishes of telescopes at a great distance. Able to see on a grand scale, oblique and accurate.

And I sat around in the desert light of that house at night, and fell asleep waiting. All the fall clocks set back to regain one lost hour. In a polka-dot dress she'd go, into the autumn night full of stars, fathoms down through the trees, to the world of streets and strangers. Random carhorns, then, in the distance. A distance at which anger sounds like longing.

Imperturbably sideways, they slide, barely grazing the rough re-
taining wall which, now and then, holds back a stray daffodil.
Adhering against all gravity, gracious and slow as a chess game in
which the pieces only seem to move at random, horned shadows
glide in and out of checkmate, where the daffodils cast themselves
huge under enchanted lamps. Pruned flat against the house and
pinned there, the pear bears freckled fruit whose flesh is white,
unworldly, grained like the tongue itself, and may be eaten as a tonic
against loneliness.

Netted in the honeycomb shadow of the light fixture, the family sat eating as though chained. The dialogue was resumed each night: those physically humiliating illnesses after which the will to survive may not survive – all dinnertable conversation veered toward that – each was taken in.

Afterwards, in our rooms, it was possible to listen twenty times in a night to the same record, incorporating the chords into gestures for getting by in the world.

Death was the unidentified guest in that house, though no place needed to be set at the table, and its sudden arrivals among us would incite the most tyrannical moods.

Other substances too may turn bittersweet: sweet potatoes, for instance, or the common carrot. Any roots, in fact, which are brought up into the light too late – or too soon.

Dark, flower-starred, it nags the memory with implausibilities. At the base of the stairs that switchback high to the lit porch it let off its fragrance, while along the eaves and under the stairs, wherever a nook allows secrecy, out of sight or out of reach, hung insect cases, mummified, between lives.

Terrible changes went on within – and still we lived in our parents' houses. Snared in that charmed circle of scent at the base of the stairs, unable to distinguish between desire and satiety. And talk! we borrowed each hour from the future. Those selves of ourselves – we behaved as though struck deaf or dumb or sightless. We lived on nothing but the imagery of the senses. Did we mean all we felt?

Jasmine still dispenses its midnight smell like an ambiguous hormone through the breath, the bloodstream, but only to frighten us with our own amnesia. What of those insects also gifted with double lives? The grey cocoons, aloof from us. As if we were not also in the chrysalis.

As if what had emerged had not lost the power of transformation.

They come at dusk down the hill to the apple trees, a few deer. They come out before stars to rub against the bark, scarring the fruit. But what deer really love to eat are roses. The moss rose they'll eat to the ground.

If you've never seen deer near the city, they move as they chew, feeding on apples, like women used to high heels and lipstick. Then they venture closer. If you love your roses you'll enclose them in cages of wire as you would a songbird.

There is the fruitless beauty of the household, and then there is the beauty of the field. Their high cheekbones as they feed on the last roses.

And that which now comes alight, the house you grew up in: sometimes it is a lantern small enough to carry before you in one hand.

III

Out on the front porch, late, the earth still emanating collective warmth. If, on a summer night, to come back is to let the vision blur, then it is not an eye for an eye, at least, but one eye superimposing upon the other the past, ghosted.

And so to come back at that slight disadvantage, not so much amnesiac, but as from long disuse, finding one has lost, almost, the ability. The need to pretend not to recognize. So much complicity.

A disused basketball hoop at midnight, kids long grown up and gone, all residential districts marked by such circles, perimeters around loss.

America is one long quarrel, and those who leave do so as through a door slammed by an angry lover, meaning to return. But there are those too with no stake in the fight.

The long low-slung cruisers mean to arouse, along the avenues, at the expense of future history, at any expense, a sentimental contempt.

To ease back into such captivity.

And to leave again?

Yes, but not tonight. Not so soon, if the leaving, too, is to be a form of bowing down.

Tonight, as often now, he takes me aside and begins to explain the details of some bodily mechanism – this time it's lipids in the blood – using the true language of that craft, covering ground we've no doubt crossed before, but skipping nothing, defining again each unfamiliar term. He remembers before I do which parts I should already know but misremember. Travelling at high speed as though through a difficult interchange and taking the wrong turnoff: that's how information is mislaid. Often, too, I've become perfectly lost in cities I've lived in for years.

A sense of direction. Stories of his driving with a passenger, deep in accompanied monologue, then abruptly stopping when the conversation ends. Having already passed the destination by up to fifty miles. There is a direction to this talk, starting at a given point and then slowly making its way round the unsuspecting listener until, within sight of the origin, the circle may be completed in a single leap. This, I am told, is the same danger big game hunters face in the wild: the tiger's wide circle through the jungle.

The topic of lipids in the blood moves on to famine, the cultural mores which, in some circumstances, preclude survival. Which foods people will eat and which ones they will not touch though it would save them. And so on.

When his children were too young to be talked to in this way, he used to sing to quiet us, which only made us cry the louder. His favorite songs: "The hipbone's connected to the – kneebone..." and "It's a Long Way to Tipperary."

There is a book he has been searching for for several years. It contains biographical sketches of men and women who performed heroically in their professions, from lighthouse-keeper in the wilds to Newton seeing the moon fall like an apple toward the earth's center. He read it at the age of seven and it caused him to take the direction he did in life. *Benefactors of the World* is no longer listed in catalogues and is unknown to experienced bookfinders in several major cities. It is possibly a pirated edition. Since early childhood he has possessed a photographic memory, but even for him seventy years is a long time to remember. If he could recall every word now he'd have no need of the book. I myself have found that the memory falters most crucially when everything depends on it, and that when you can't locate the book you need you must find the way to bring it into being.

Dad in his chair snoozing in the only patch of warmth and brightness this side of the equator, the protective cone of the reading lamp. His terrycloth robe dangling strings, orange peels going ancient among butts in an ashtray the size of a dinnerplate which he has commanded us never to empty. Home late I tiptoe through, the TV distorted at twice the normal volume so it's impossible to hear, the treadmill of frames skipping over known faces performing *normal* as they try to step out of their terrified haloes wholly outlined, the control bar tilting in his hand. Touch anything and he'd wake instantly; the twentieth century is his child. He'll ask me to sit and massage his toes, his wrists, and tell him a story, a good one, something about the world . . . then drift between the words and away. No matter how gently I ease off, he's awake. Always a third eye on the sounds, the rhythms, whatever lullaby surrounds him.

These are the scenes replayed so often they are known by heart, moving as though by remote control.

Often I come in to find them both asleep, mammoths preserved in the icy light of the TV, the sound punched off since the last commercial they could hear, hours, eons ago.

MOSTLY IT IS THE FUTURE WHICH
HAUNTS THIS HOUSE

On the hill the great house cannot sleep. Into the huge abandoned living room, stray headlights stream like malformed pearls, jettisoned. Upstairs the windows, clear of the unconscious breath of sleepers, yield nothing. And the house's heart sinks, the heater igniting its echo in each room, for all it continues to protect with its mechanical warmth.

Through the basement frosty with dust, through the tinselled cracks in glass, outside the garden has grown wild and rangy. The beast returning to its loneliness when beauty forsakes it.

Mostly what weeps are the raw bright fruits of the city night. Blue haze among the basement tools, smoke of half a century that does not disperse but clings among the silent stands of drill-bits, the Waltzing Matilda lathe. Among the foundations of childhood, where the units of measure are calculated, behind the face behind the cigarette between my father's lips.

Earth orchid and angel's trumpet. Watsonia, the honey flower.

Among mops which lean their dirt-grey hair, their hidden eyes, between kitchen door and camellias.

Among other tall tools.

Beneath pittosporum branches, the black leather droppings and acrid seed.

Ollieollieoxenfree. Echoes down the blue canyon evening streets.

Sunshadows on fallen oak leaves. Taunting, *come and get me*.

Until all have discovered, in dreams, the secret wing of the house.

Black summer night, volcanic with flowers, ashen. Lizards that jet across the path and then cling with small claws to the trees. Stilled pendulums of the passion vine. Against the undersurface of the pond goldfish croon, panning with their lips for food, and a frog can steady itself on a pad, startling a flock of lilies. The strobed ripples. The bare breeze. America, on the ninth of June, inoculating its sleepers with the myth. Entering the breath.

And the suction of that snore! The moth shivering in the hot bright lamp. The book clamped by a hand, unread but open to the page and to the chest. In and out, swung higher, farther: as far as the breath can take us with closed eyes. The great south face of the house, uncontested. Washed up in windowglass: a coconut moon.

After dark the flowers let their other scent into the air, as if thinking aloud. Wild roses, magenta and white, the white ones their furred ghosts. And the wheedling music of the insects, planning a city that was never meant to come to fruition in daylight. What dreamers they are. And yet, just listening to them, that glittering bank of lights comes back: whatever city you imagined first, in childhood, as the way in or out.

We went, didn't we, each of us, after something. Like a dog running after a stick which was nothing more than the faked motion of his master's throwing arm. We lost what we couldn't remember. We lost our intentions.

The stars approach, but only so near they don't ground themselves on the shallows. They let their cargo be unloaded from them. And what cargo they carried, back in those days! The hotel, white as an iced cake among the palms. The palms, their bark that fell away like netting, the fronds we'd find like huge whips on the ground after a storm.

All night the pines grow electric with insect noise: enough power for a whole city. But the barest beginning of dawn shuts them down, so the insects wait in silence and limbo beneath the bark as another personality takes over the earth. One with a baby blue sky and the pines twisted against it in the shapes of our old, powerful, outmoded longings.

A NOTE ON THE TEXT

For readers unfamiliar with the setting of these poems, some background may be useful. Berkeley and Oakland are situated on the eastern shore of San Francisco Bay. From the poet's childhood home, in the hilly outskirts of Berkeley, one looked down to the left on Oakland (an industrial port city), to the right on Berkeley (a university town), and straight across the bay to San Francisco.

*

The author expresses gratitude to the Canada Council and the Ontario Arts Council for their material support; and to Dennis Lee for his not immaterial enthusiasm.

Also to those journals in which these poems first appeared: *Athanor; The Canadian Forum; Canadian Literary Review; Canadian Literature; Dandelion; Ethos; Event; Fireweed; Four By Four; Island; NeWest Review; Quarry; Raddle Moon; Toronto Life; Waves; The Literary Half-Yearly* (India). "Rain" and "Spring" first appeared in *American Poetry Review*.

An excerpt from "Folklore" won first prize for poetry in the Canadian Broadcasting Corporation's 1982 literary competition, and was broadcast on the CBC.